CW00863745

PASSPORT TO MASCULINITY

PASSPORT TO MASCULINITY

From Boyhood to Male Adulthood

The Art of Mentoring Men

BELMONT F. HAYDEL, PhD

To order additional copies of this book, contact:
Xlibris
844-714-8691
www.Xlibris.com
Orders@Xlibris.com
824676

CONTENTS

Dedication

To the Memory
of
My Beloved Ancestral-Parents

Belmont and Elmira Brown Haydel (parents)

Willie and Stella Bennette Brown (paternal grandparents)

Thomas and Mary Seals Brown
(paternal great-grandparents)

Elphege and Josephine Honoré Haydel
(maternal grandparents)

Martin Joseph and Emesie Chessé Honoré
(maternal great-grandparents)

Preface

Often, we writers ask ourselves what prompts us to engage in a desired topic or even what we may initially perceive to be the topic. While I should acknowledge that "there is nothing new under the sun" (Ecclesiastes 1:9), I cannot speak for other writers but only for myself, as I recognize that this book does not purport to add to any divergent sunray. In my books and other professional writings, I have always known my motivations clearly in advance, thus elevating my ambitions to a God-bestowed voice saying, "Do it now." I believe I am contributing to society with further information on this evolving interchange between male mentors and male mentees. Time will be a measuring rod of my contributions in this field. My nonacademic and professional writings are historical, inspirational, and prognostic. This book is not expected to be an empirical set of facts; rather, it is intended to provide information by using methodology that examines facts through the involvement of selected participants.

"No man is an island," I believe, is an underlying treatise of my book on mentoring young men. My selected mentees reside on my treasured "island," for they are a part of me and I am a part of them. Perhaps this book is merely a reflection of my own past, as I endeavor to conduct my introspection related to the male gender. My emphasis reveals that all of us men are but grown-up boys, or maybe the reverse that we are boys growing up, regardless of environment, genetics, or any other accidentals that impact masculinity. Thus, boys will be boys as they become men without recognizing their childhood and teenage lives; perhaps I should just say *harvesting men*. In addition, there will always be trials in life (St. Augustine's *Confessions*).

In writing this book, I find myself led by this premise in attempting to understand myself through observing other men, although this latter thought is not the principal reason for my research. In reading this book, one may divine my motivation without my trying to describe it. Not only is this work mainly designed to be inspirational for young men to further develop their masculinity and to clarify why and who boys and men are, but it can also be used in academic settings.

Note that like any other living animal, the human male is complex and often difficult to define anthropologically, biologically, socially, historically, environmentally, or in any other scientific application. Surely, as a male, I have discovered that boys and men are an interconnected set, differing only by age and time. As years passed and I grew older, I realized the impact of experience and exposure on who I am today.

The Contents and Introduction reveal, in part, where this book will carry the reader. In the introduction, I explain some details about the contents, including the underlying rationale for each subtopic. The Commentaries after each chapter represent my conclusions along with personal reflections.

The book does not approach the myriad of the subject of mentoring, as this socially interactive behavior between mentors and mentees does not fall within my professional realm. I respectfully acknowledge that my thoughts are my own interpretation with which I do not expect the experts to concur. Logically then, my views do not necessarily show professional expertise, at least as psychologists know them, but are based heavily on my own experiences with young men and their growing-up processes. Likewise, I do not consider my views as professional additions to the literature, as these observations are mostly my impressions. Yet I have examined much scholarly works that have influenced my academics. Most of all, I have deliberately tried to make a difference through this work.

In preparing this book, I have earnestly tried not to present myself as a dedicated mentor but hopefully possessing humble reality for benefits to my mentees. Although some names of my selected mentees have not been included in my narrative, I have respectfully acknowledged all contributing persons, some of whom should not be interpreted as mentees. Thus, I also believe the impact should likely impress the audience as a genuine contribution to the development of our society.

My story is neither fable nor fiction, as it began with my mentoring young men. As a 2nd Lieutenant in a US Army Infantry company consisting of 197 young soldiers at Ft. Carson, Colorado, in 1954, where my principal duty was training soldiers in basic infantry strategies, which also included 4.2″ mortar education and training. Additionally, I was assigned as Defense Counsel; therefore, I had to familiarize myself with the Uniform Code of Military Justice (UCMJ). I was battered with the problems of young soldiers, which was not my task nor my intention as military officer. This activity began my mentoring experience; these memories consume me even today.

I have never asked for nor have I ever received any financial compensation for my mentoring efforts. Among my most interesting experiences was my surprise appointment in 1989 to the position as Executive Director of the Inter-American Center (IAC) of Loyola University of New Orleans, by Father Louis Twomey, the director of the university's Institute of Human Relations. One of my duties was negotiating the funding of the IAC with the federal government, which included my interactions with Dr. Henry Kissinger and Alexander Haig, along with Louisiana's Congressional National Delegation, namely Congressman Edward Hebert and Senators Allen J. Ellender and Russell B. Long. I suppose these rewarding experiences were ordained by the will and grace of God.

In the words of Cardinal John Newman, "God has created me to do Him some definite services ... Therefore, I will trust Him." I honestly believe Almighty God is my creator, and He alone is my final destiny.

Foreword

This book is a microcosm of seventy years of the ninety years that Belmont Haydel has lived as friend, confidant, and mentor to more boys and men that we can count. It presents just a taste of Belmont's energy and patience, along with his ultimate desire to share the flavors of life that permeate his own as he takes the hand of each male mentee who is reaching for future success and happiness.

I have watched a magnetism that exists when my husband reaches out to young men who are searching for a path, yet uncovered, that can lead them to achieving their potentials. Intuitively, he finds their heart when they have yet to discover it. His guidance reveals his understanding, based on his religious convictions, that for each individual the difference between the right and the wrong path is not fixed, not absolute; the way may change over time as young men begin to mature.

A true Renaissance Man, Belmont has demonstrated in this book his perception that all young men should attempt to fully develop their God-given capacities through embracing knowledge. He extends his hand and creates a *reach*, a connection that cannot be ignored, one that carries his mentees beyond their degree of comfort to a new level of awareness. When he meets a man, regardless of age, he connects on multiple levels and detects within that person a masculine root that he helps to grow.

Nina J. Haydel, EdD

Mentoring is the brain to pick, an ear to
listen, and a push in the right direction.
—John C. Crosby

Introduction

My book follows a long-intentioned desire to fulfill a dream or passion wrapped around values of masculinity. In my early years (under twenty), I never sought the task of mentoring young men, which has mounted over the years of my life to include those men who were getting older, in midlife (I refer to those over forty-five). Throughout my own aging process, I have learned that by gaining experience and knowledge, boys grow into a stronger sense of masculinity, although some believe they already know it all; as such, those youngsters already consider themselves men. You will see these distinctions in Chapter 3. My major purpose in writing this book is to motivate mentees; in other words, to inspire them.

Who are mentors and what is mentoring? As these topics are varied and dependent on whose definitions are applicable, I offer these descriptions: "Mentoring is more like giving and receiving rather than simply understanding" (Wicks, 2000). My own version describes mentoring as the experience of giving of self or sharing oneself with others. Most of the time, my mentees would seek my advice, as they could depend on me.

My mentees have included young army adults, various professionals, diplomats, foreign and US government officials, college students, and family members; only a few have been politicians. I have never focused on their race, skin color, religion, age, sexual preference, or any other human accident. My attention rested on their personal needs; likewise, I have considered myself equipped to accommodate their concerns and ambitions. My mentoring universe includes approximately forty late-teenage boys as well as multiple matured men.

Proudly, I have learned much more from my mentees than I have given them. Surely, I could never keep up with all of them. I shared their significant celebrations, such as weddings, children's christenings, bar and bat mitzvahs, and graduations. On one occasion, I sadly delivered the eulogy at the funeral of a beloved fraternity brother. These events that peppered my life remind me of Shakespeare's quote: "All the world's a stage, and all men and women merely players."

In preparing this book, my research carried me deep into scholarly volumes and sources related to many subtopics: male behaviors, ages, professions, values, religions, languages, and cultures. Nonetheless, most of my thoughts herein about mentees have come from my experiences with them throughout many years.

Lastly, the story of my mentoring begins with my adult and professional life after my graduation from Loyola University of Chicago in 1953. Therefore, in this book I do not write about my childhood and teenage experiences. However, I strongly believe that my early formative years have had a major impact on the later years of my life.

I am not a teacher, but an awakener.

—*Robert Frost*

Chapter I

Author's Mentors

Acknowledgment of My Mentors: How They Influenced My Behavior

My memories related to the men described below represent their legacies that reside in my life.

George Aschenbrenner, SJ, Spiritual Director, Jesuit Center for Spiritual Direction, Wernersville, Pennsylvania:

In 1993, on the occasion of my attending a Catholic retreat at the magnificent medieval castle in Wernersville, Pennsylvania, I met Father George Aschenbrenner. I had often followed the teaching of the Order of the Jesuits and found solace in the Father's words and ideas. He and I shared spirituality that rested on his background and advanced theological knowledge with an emphasis on the virtue of humility. He filled my purpose: spiritual direction and guidance, much like my visiting a psychologist but with the will of God. We spent numerous hours discussing my career plans and future endeavors that followed my retirement from the Faculty of Business Administration at Rider University in 1994.

Belmont Haydel Sr., florist, real estate business executive, entrepreneur, and a contemporary Haydel family devotee:

My father was a spark that ignited my life of service to mankind. His family nickname was *Bonbon* (Good, Good in Creole French), illustrating his good nature. From the time I was a youngster, I watched him treat people with dignity and care, regardless of who they were. He provided monetary assistance, advice, business suggestions, and empathy, never turning anyone away. As I watched him in his real estate and retail businesses, I learned from his negotiation skills and his business acumen. His demonstration of patience as he taught me techniques of flower arranging and strategies for success in retailing encouraged and inspired me in developing my skills and interests, later leading me to my future professions. He fostered my interest in advanced academic studies and always supported my decisions while advising me in difficult situations. Along with my father's examples, I learned to love and respect mankind. In many ways, my father was also a subconscious mentor to those who knew and observed him.

Alton McDonald, dentist, psychologist, New Orleans, Louisiana:

Dr. McDonald, my mother's dentist, did more than drill my mother's teeth; he offered me his expertise based on his secondary career as a psychologist. He had received a degree in psychology from a university in Mexico.

This Latin American connection was forged while I sat in his living room listening to his experiences about his studying in Mexico and how he felt it could enrich my life. He had also traveled throughout Central America, and his experiences whetted my appetite for enjoying that part of the world. Living in Louisiana gave both of us a special attachment to the land just south of our border. I took his career advice very seriously, which set me on my path to studying in Mexico City. Following my entrance into the professional world in Latin America, whenever I returned to Louisiana, I visited Dr. McDonald to recount my experiences and lean on his psychological expertise related to my questions and concerns.

William Lytle Schurz, PhD, diplomat, educator, professor of Latin American studies, renown author and scholar, president and professor of American Institute for Foreign Trade, Glendale, Arizona:

As a student at the American Institute for Foreign Trade in 1957, I attended a class on Latin America taught by a famous economic historian, Dr. William Schurz. He had been a commercial attaché to Brazil under the Hoover Administration and was known for his works on Latin American history, particularly Brazil. While seated in the audience of sixty or so students in the lecture hall, I heard Dr. Schurz calling my name and asking me to meet him at his office after class. I had never spoken to him individually, as in a class that size, his graduate assistants oversaw student interaction and academic assessment. I had no idea how he knew of me. He said the following: "Take my class next semester on Brazil. Brazil needs you and you need Brazil." I relied on his suggestions and followed his directions. His words were prophetic. Surprisingly, his counseling and foresight became a reality when President John F. Kennedy gave me a diplomatic appointment in 1963. Within four weeks after President Kennedy's assassination on November 22, 1963, President Lyndon B. Johnson assigned me to Brazil as a foreign service officer (diplomat), leading me to Rio de Janeiro on January 3, 1964. After an intensive six-week study of the Portuguese language in the American Embassy building, I moved into my own office, a room on the fourth floor of the Embassy, which may have held the ghost of Dr. Schurz. I often felt his presence as I began my work as a young economist. The rest is history.

Louis Twomey, SJ, PhD, professor and director of the Institute of Human Relations at Loyola University of New Orleans, Louisiana:

In early 1969, after I returned to Louisiana from my State Department posts, within the week, I received a telephone call from the chairman of the Economics Department of Tulane University on behalf of Father Twomey, the current director of the institute. He was looking for a replacement for director of the Inter-American Center, a department of Loyola's Institute. I had casually met Father Twomey through a mutual friend in 1961. Our meeting led him to invite me to accept the position as the university's second executive, Director of the Inter-American Center, which had received a grant from the US Agency for International Development with the purpose of indoctrinating young potential Latin American leaders with sensitivity training along with substantive courses in economics and political science. Many of these apprentices later became contributory leaders in their respective countries. Father Twomey's impact on me, based on his views and practice in social justice, spearheaded my performance in securing funding from the US government, supervising all activities and employees, and traveling through Latin America to interview the participants for the center's programs. Father Twomey was a true humanitarian, a God-fearing individual. His influence resonated with me and allowed me to further my career as a humanitarian.

Commentary

The background of these five men and their influence on me have led me to live, on a conscious level, as a mentor for others. For my mentors above, I pray Almighty God's blessing on them with His eternal rewards.

If you light a lamp for someone, it will
also brighten your own path.

—*Buddhist Proverb*

Chapter II

Elements of Masculinity

Traditionally, *masculinity* is often confused with or is synonymous with *manhood*. There are many definitions of both terms. In my discussions with my mentees, we have never engaged in discussing the difference between these two concepts. There may be cultural realms that offer distinctions, such as religions, environments, male images, ages, and parental behaviors.

By *masculinity*, I have endeavored to present boys growing up from male adolescents to male maturity. *Masculinity* may be construed to mean many things.

A dictionary's definition reports that *masculinity* belongs only to the male person, never to the female, whereas *manhood* relates to humans or the human family, both male and female and together collectively.

Metaphorically, when a boy climbs a ladder moving upward, he will encounter difficult steps; but as he approaches the top of the ladder, he finds stronger masculinity. Here, masculinity becomes a reality. Even before reaching the high levels of maturity "in the preschoolers' life is the television set, which is arguably the bearer of the worst messages about masculinity" (Newberger, p. 101). This concept often affects a child negatively. The power of TV shapes early values of young children through "quick-moving images, small bites, [little] thoughtful commentaries, and explanations" (p. 102). Often, there are dramatizations of relationships and punishments that affect the perceptions of male power and the perceptions of the masculine effect on others. These visions influence children's reactions to powerful messages exhibited by the male figures they see on the screen.

Masculinity to me means being responsible and dependable. Leadership abilities is a significant component of masculinity and kindness to others, no matter who they are or their position in society. Finally, an awareness pervades a male when he sees his future as the head of a family at some point.

Toxic Masculinity

Men often respect the concept of masculinity regarding positive characteristics. Unfortunately, many times they are unaware that negative behaviors dominate the elements of their own masculine tendencies. We look at that as having toxic masculine traits that serve a harmful purpose, traits that are destructive or poisonous in nature. *Toxic masculinity* is a term used in academia to refer to behaviors related to certain cultural norms that can be associated with harm to men as well as to society. I suggest that mentees seek therapy as resolution to toxic behavior. A component of toxic behavior is connected to traditional stereotypes that show men as socially dominant, presenting their behaviors through related traits, such as misogyny and homophobia, that can promote violence and sexual assault. These negative aspects of exaggerated masculine traits have been accepted, embraced, and even glorified by many cultures. This harmful concept of masculinity also places significant importance on *manliness* based on strength, lack of emotion, self-sufficiency, dominance, and sexuality. In my experience in mentoring men, I have never witnessed any toxic behavior.

Mentees' Views of Masculinity

I designed the questionnaire and distributed it to my mentees in search of their views related to numerous concepts and their perceptions. The following quotes verbalize their personal reflections on the term *masculinity*:

- "It means thinking, acting, and being aware of the differences between men, biological sexes, and people, but more so sensitivity towards those differences. It also means for men to be mindful and careful in employing strength and power over others." Anonymous

- "As a product of a single sex, male Catholic school, my definition of masculinity is very much influenced by one's experience and training. Masculinity to me means being responsible and dependable. Leadership abilities is a significant component of masculinity and being kind to others, no matter who they are or their position in society, finally, knowing that you have the responsibility to lead the family at one point." Ruben Armiñana

- "To me masculinity is the essence of maleness, and there-in lies the problem: It is impossible to define (in words) the essence of anything. I had a professor decades ago that would challenge me to define the essence of any object of my choosing, even inanimate objects like 'a door.' The clue is that the definition must explain what makes a door a door and not something else, as that is the essence of a door, by definition. No matter what definition I came up with, he would prove me wrong. I learned the game, so I can play too; believe me, it is impossible to win, i.e., is impossible to come up with the definition of the essence of a door and yet, when you are in front of one, you know it's a door. I think one way to look at what you are asking is precisely that, 'masculinity is the essence of maleness,' which allows you to know that the individual is a male when you are in front of one. So far, the answer sounds more in the field of philosophy than biology, right? Well … wait; it's going to be down to chromosomes and hormones (mainly)." Dr. Hernán Baldassarre

• Translated from Portuguese: "Masculinity—Today there is a complete concept that defines GENDER or a biological double balance. Therefore, masculinity depends on paternal biology and culture that, in turn, further depends on a series of one's viewpoint. Regarding being a male in Brazil and its Latin culture, masculinity is linked to being primarily perceived by the opposite sex, as demonstrating libido or desire. With this point of view, it is viewed as the process of moving on from adolescence or producing testosterone or discovering libido. As a perceived concept, to be macho, we depend on one's viewpoint or maybe on culture which defines hope. In Brazilian culture, masculinity is linked to desires about sex in such a manner that relates to an intense search for a dynamic partner. There exists a big difference in the semantics about the ideas of masculinity and maturity, which are different concepts and may combine to become a cultural process." Haller Freitas

- "Masculinity is a form of identity, generally associated with strength and power. Masculinity is not just physical power but courage and toughness. Traditionally, masculinity was associated with men, but it has been transformed and can be associated with both men and women." Anonymous

- Mentee, a former practicing psychologist and mentor himself, shares an extensive commentary about his experience and concept of masculinity:

"When I hear the word 'masculinity,' what image instantly comes to mind? I see some kind of action-hero, like on a movie poster. He has enormous muscles, a stern but confident look, perhaps combat gear, maybe high-tech weaponry, and is definitely larger than life. In his Schwarzenegger-like pose, he's ready to take on any villain or threat. He looks massively strong and invincible. And, women like him [*sic*].

"This hypermacho version of masculinity may seem a little juvenile, but that's what I see if I'm honest. This brings questions of how I was raised, not just by my parents, but also the influences of media during the sixties (Superman, TV Batman, John Wayne, sports figures) and the words of my coaches, physical education teachers, and peer group. What kinds of games did we play as young boys versus those played by the girls? What were boys told about not being cry-babies, sissies, wimps, and wussies? (And worse, laugh.) How often did I feel shame about not quite measuring up when it came to sports, dating, and all of that? And what did I do to compensate growing up? Feeling shame is an incredibly painful experience that also motivates.

"To understand and define masculinity, there must be a contrast with femininity. The first image that pops into my head for femininity is a beautiful young woman with long tan legs in a pretty dress with floral prints, maybe nature or pastels in the background, along with submissive posturing. It's important to note that she's not overweight. Despite my education and life experiences about the changing roles for women and the power they possess, I'm being honest. At least the young woman I see is not bent over naked, right?

"It's difficult for any of us to be totally free from traditional stereotypes when we consume current-day media and advertising. Women on newscasts tend to be younger and better looking than their male counterparts. Movies are still criticized for old men acting opposite very young women. Maybe it's not all the fault of men. Perhaps women too want to see a youthful representation of their gender. I don't mean this offensively, and I know plenty of women absolutely reject that idea or ideal and are unhappy with modern portrayals.

"So, how do I define masculinity today if I give it more thought? That's tough for me. I see this issue of gender differences becoming less relevant in modern life.

"As a child, I saw careers open only to men that helped define masculinity for that time. In the sixties, we rarely knew of women who were doctors, lawyers, corporate leaders, politicians, airline pilots, accountants, police officers, or even mail carriers. Women were preferably mothers at home or in some cases secretaries, receptionists, elementary school teachers, and members of other 'less important' occupations. But then the women's liberation movement caught fire in the sixties, and that brought dramatic change. As the father of two adult daughters, I'm proud of not only what they've become but the opportunities afforded to them.

"Of course, you still see gender differences in professions. Women do not tend to be professional football players, construction workers, or carry the heavy furniture when you call a moving company.

Physical differences and brute strength naturally come into play. But many, many barriers have been broken just in my lifetime. That doesn't even take into account women's right to vote and lots of other constraints on gender roles and freedoms requiring a struggle throughout American history.

"As an aside and a little off topic, the 19th Amendment is interesting because I asked my father whether or not he thought my grandmother was excited when she got the right to vote as a young woman in 1920, when it was ratified by Congress. He said, 'I don't think so.' Dad explained that she would not have felt comfortable voting because it was still considered unacceptable in her rural southern community. When I knew her, my grandmother was always a big proponent of voting and seemed like a very strong woman. The years and shifting culture have really changed us.

"The other issue muddying the traditional masculinity waters is our society's relatively recent recognition of

LGBTQ rights. 'Queer' was one of those bad words you didn't want to be called when you were a boy growing up, and there were far worse words, as we all know. Males often felt the need to prove their heterosexuality. You didn't want to do anything that might make people wonder or start rumors. Besides considered shameful, practicing same-sex love was actually an illegal activity in the not-so-distance past.

"Looking at today's political conservativism as it relates to masculinity, I suppose I fall short because I have never owned a gun. I do know women who love going to firing ranges and practice 'conceal and carry,' so it's not just a masculine thing. But I do wonder for men how much of their political conservative posturing is an attempt to project masculinity. I have good friends who are quite conservative politically and based on their comments, right-wing politics often equals manliness. To be macho, it helps to own lots of assault-style weapons and vote for certain candidates who talk tough and use combative, divisive language.

"For me, masculinity means that I enjoy dressing as a man, being complimented by women, and being the leader in a shared hobby with my wife, ballroom dancing. I sometimes joke that's about the only time I'm a leader with her (not really true). We share chores around the house, but my wife still does almost all of the laundry out of fear I might not do it right. And she's the one who asks, 'So how many days have you worn those jeans?' I'm not always truthful with that question, (laugh). Maybe masculinity involves sloppiness.

"I enjoy being the one asked to do any heavy lifting by the women at my business. I joke that it's the one time at work I can be a man. I enjoy opening doors for women, but in recent years I think I'm more inclined to do that for men as well (maybe without as much flair). I also like it when women open doors for me, and I'm quick to compliment them for it. Kindness to everyone is much more important than gender roles. Humanity triumphs masculinity or femininity, in my opinion.

"In any dangerous situation where I'm the only man, or one of a few, I hope that I would be brave and willing to risk my life, for other men too, of course, but especially for women. That's not been tested fortunately, but I believe I would come through. This seems like a masculine expectation and duty. I'm not sure how many other masculine duties are left, and that could just be my ignorance. Masculinity is bravery for sure, at least in my head.

"I think masculinity becomes truly relevant when men interact with their significant others. Do we show respect? Do we listen? Or at least strive to improve how we do these things? Do we empathize without trying to fix everything? Do we really try to be sensitive and seek to understand what women want in the bedroom and everywhere? I believe that's where a new kind of masculinity becomes important and essential to healthy relationships. Yes, I'm redefining masculinity for myself to include sensitivity to the opposite sex.

"Another way masculinity plays out in my life is at social gatherings for couples. The men and women do tend to congregate in separate groups. I will, however, sometimes catch myself listening in on what the women are saying because their topics are sometimes more interesting to me. That's okay.

"I think that also in my life there has been real value in being mentored by other men. I'm not sure that I would always have gotten the same experiences and insights with women. Sexual attractions can develop, not always, but I've seen times when they do and that clouds things. I've even experienced older women developing a fondness for me that I was unsure exactly how to interpret. Not always. But having male mentors has really helped me grow as a person and as a business leader. I've learned a lot about my own leadership and creativity. The mentoring situations with other males that have proved most useful have involved understanding the world and how to make a difference in the lives of others. And if I'm honest, how to make money. I just have not learned those things as much from women for whatever reason.

"In mentoring young men, especially those I employed and supervised, I hope that I instilled a sense of dedication, honesty, and perseverance in reaching goals. Some of the men who have worked for me went on to earn remarkable achievements. One has become quite famous internationally, one of the top game creators, and I'm always flattered when he pays me a visit. I have influenced women too, including my daughters. Typically, in the workplace, I have spent more time with young men, perhaps because that's less likely to raise suspicions. And maybe there is something distinctive in the way men mentor other men that's more effective. I'll leave that one to the experts.

"Although a lot has changed over the decades and we are a more gender-neutral society, I never want to sound dismissive of the importance of masculinity in my modern-day personal life. Male and female are still what make the world go around. Sexuality is a huge deal. Entertainment that celebrates the feminine form can be exciting and pleasurable when not excessive or disrespectful. I know biology does play a role even though masculine socialization is not the same as it once was. Though I'm not totally aware of every aspect of my masculine identity and how it influences my thoughts and behavior, there's absolutely no question; I enjoy being a man." Richard Caudel

Commentary

These perceptions of masculinity are a major part of my mentees' defining what they perceive as maleness, an inherent part of themselves. These may be projections of self and internal mirrors that comfort the male psyche. It is interesting to note that in her article "The Miseducation of the American Boy," Peggy Orenstein described the definition of the term *masculinity* that mirrored my collection of descriptions. She validates my findings as well that only 2 percent of her sample of male respondents felt that honesty and morality were significant traits. Thus, the development of young men can be ascribed to their years of experience that hopefully enables them to further contribute to society.

Adversity toughens manhood, and the characteristic
of the good or the great man is not that he has been
exempt from the evils of life, but that he has
surmounted them.
—*Patrick Henry*

Chapter III
Summary of Mentees' Revelations

Introduction

As I remember those commemorative years involving my personal relationships with young males and older adult males, ages eighteen through seventy-five, delightfully, my heart is full. I am now celebrating these unforgettable years, although with heartfelt sorrow, as I recall former mentees who have passed on to their eternal rest. *Requiescat in pace* (may they rest in peace).

I created and distributed a questionnaire to some forty-five mentees, giving them an opportunity to contemplate the factual essence of their lives and resurrect the events that have no doubt been buried in their years since childhood. Their responses are the base for my understanding of how demographics and critical events can impact the success of a relationship between male mentors and their mentees. Analysis of the impact of the multiple events will follow in Chapter 4. I am neither a statistician nor professional researcher, but I found the information from my mentee universe worthy of reporting, as these demographics reveal who my mentees are and how they responded to many first-person musings about their pasts.

Demographics

Nationalities and Ethnicities

I found an interesting mix of backgrounds although most of my mentees have been Caucasians. They have come from the following national origins: US American, German, Hungarian, Irish, Italian, Cuban, English, French, Paraguayan, Peruvian, Brazilian, and Ecuadorian. Ethnic categories include Hispanic, Palestinian, Slavic, Quechua Indians (Peru), and Guarani Indians (Paraguay). I will consider the impact in Chapter 4, "Analysis."

Foreign Languages

All mentees know perfect English; several speak French, Portuguese, Arabic, and Guarani (native Paraguay Indian language). Many of them are bilingual, several trilingual, and two are quadrilingual (my Paraguayan mentees). I was able to communicate in several languages, in addition to my native tongue, English.

Religions

Most mentees belong to the following faiths: Protestantism, Roman Catholicism, Judaism, and Islamism. Feelings and behaviors varied with regard to their practice of their faiths: Several only practiced religions on holidays with family; others reported totally rejecting religion in their early years. Here, I paraphrase how several mentees verbalized their reflections:

1. While growing up, religion made him feel guilty or unworthy; this resulted in his diminished

self-confidence. Once he claimed he was a pragmatic Catholic; he thought of organized religion as a "pyramid scheme" of control.

2. Sometimes religion impacted his behavior and his interests positively.

3. Still, as an adult, he has little interest in Catholicism although he was raised a Catholic.

4. Several thought that God could be truly found in all things.

Family Structure

Most adult mentees' families consisted of one to five children, both male and female. Some couples had only biological offspring, but I found several couples with both adopted and biological children, while a few had only adopted children. Fewer than ten couples had no children. In addition, several were blended families following remarriage, thus adding the count of up to ten children.

Personal Reflections

Personality

In reflecting upon their personalities, during their early youth, some mentees reported themselves as being extremely shy. A few considered themselves introverts. Based on these personality identifiers, several answers to my questionnaire regarding early memories are as follows:

1. "As a teenager, most of my school and religious interests grew while beginning to appreciate my elders."
2. "In my boyhood years, initially I was shy, but stable. I grew out of shyness, as I began to mingle with adult boys."
3. "I was a typical boy around ages 7–8; I became a Boys Scout at age 7."
4. "I was fundamentally stable, between the ages 7–15 or so, characterized as introvert at school."
5. "I was inclined to like math and science in school. I was an Altar Boy and blessed with stable male friends who have remained most of my life for over

40 years. As I have been athletic most of my life, but as a young adult naturally I was more active in sports."

6. "I was shy, rational; good student, somewhat social; always extrovert; I enjoyed companionship."

7. "As a teenager, my most school and religious interests and relationship with elders and peers constituted my life; I was psychologically shy, a typical boy around ages 7–8, and a Boys Scout; I was fundamentally stable between ages 7–15; in school I was characterized as an introvert; liked math and science; I was an Altar Boy."

These memories led to considerable conversations with me and further mentee introspection.

Mistakes and Regrets

Based on self-reflection, we all acknowledge that our lives twist and turn as we make decisions, sometimes in error. Although mistakes can be viewed as failures, they are often a learning tool that can serve as an awakening that provides positive development and future success. In addition, this small sampling reveals the level of importance some men place on varied experiences. The mentees reflected on their mistakes:

1. He took many chances in business that caused failures, but he does not consider any of these experiences regrettable.

2. His first marriage was to his childhood sweetheart. She was having severe behavioral and psychological problems, but he thought he could handle it because he loved her. She needed counseling when they started life together. After seven years of marriage, when he returned from the Air Force, he learned she was unfaithful; this relationship with another man resulted in the birth of an illegitimate child whom he accepted as his own. Later, he and his first wife divorced. He enjoyed relationships with several other women over the years until he decided to remarry. That marriage endured for twenty years and later resulted in a second divorce. These traumas caused him great sorrow. His mentor, after serious discussions, offered him further counsel and

friendship and suggested he seek professional help. Now at the age of fifty, he has regained emotional stability.

3. He neglected to make his marriage and family a priority, but after his fraternity adviser convinced him through a religious retreat, he became a better person with his family.

4. His biggest regret is not going to see Elvis (Presley) in concert … which was less than five months before Presley died (presumably the distance was too far from where he was living in 1977).

Catastrophic Situations

Many mentees have admitted that they had experienced or witnessed catastrophes:

1. The mentee's step-grandson was born with just one hand.

2. He experienced the early death of both parents, forcing him to grow up and become a stronger person.

3. As a former TV reporter in Central America, he witnessed hurricanes and earthquakes that caused great devastation and poverty.

4. When Kuwait was invaded by Iraq in 1990, he was terrified and bewildered as he escaped with his family.

5. The passing of his father, although it had been many years, caused him much grief, but he continues to remember his father's cherished care.

6. He experienced significant grief in dealing with the death of his best buddy's son.

Inhibitors

This sampling reveals what mentees have acknowledged exhibited inhibiting factors that have influenced their behaviors:

- Several mentees revealed they misunderstood or had no interest in different races and personalities.
- He is not willing to accept any changes in life.
- Too often he engages in excessive use of alcohol and playing video games.

Many psychological restrictions related to personal fears as well as emotional and sexual relationships.

Personality

My mentees revealed multiple types of personalities. Many claimed to be introverted, while others were extroverted. A few confessed to have been egotistical as youngsters but did not consider that as part of their present personality. My descriptions analyzed in Chapter 4 represent their range of personalities, both perceived and real.

Education

Elementary and Secondary Levels

Although my mentees were well past their primary school education, they offered reflections and perceptions of themselves at a younger age. In high school, many were open-minded and liked most subjects, yet others reported they found school boring and mundane and did not do well. One reported he had the highest GPA in high school. Several referred to having caring, talented elementary school teachers they would never forget.

Post–High School Levels

My mentees reported their achieving a wide range of college and university degrees:

- BS/BA, major in marketing and management, with a minor in international business
- BS in telecommunications after the year 2010
- undergraduate degree in electrical engineering
- BS in psychology
- MBA in human resource administration
- MBA in business administration
- MS in school psychology
- MBA in entrepreneurial studies
- PhD in political science
- PhD in clinical psychology
- doctoral degrees in law and management in Paraguay

Cultural Activities

I have tried to gauge my mentees' cultural activities but without much success because they had not shown any significant affinity to what I consider cultural activities. Several mentees enjoy reading, and some listen to popular music. Several said they have attended live performances of drama and musicals. One mentee valued attending live performances while in Europe. Another, the president of a university, said he participated in the building of a $200 million concert hall that is now internationally acclaimed. Some mentees said they had seen cultural performances in renowned/famous theaters. Another reported he took part in intellectual activities, but he did not identify them. My Paraguayan mentees were very fond of their native Spanish/Guarani Indian music that was played on harps and sung in both languages.

Contributions to Society

Almost all mentees have made contribution of one sort or another. This is just a sampling of what several mentees described:

- One mentee stated that his influence on thirteen nieces and nephews has contributed to their active participation in their communities.
- As a professional engineer, he has mentored younger engineers and other professional colleagues.

- With active involvement with his fraternity brothers, he has boosted their spirit, and his strong participation with his fraternity pledges have contributed to their success.

- Another fraternity brother feels that working with younger boys has contributed to their future outlook.

Greatest Achievements

Interestingly, the mentees claimed their professional, rather than their personal accomplishments as most important. Some 85 percent of my mentees have university degrees. Five percent have been (many still are) university professors.

Hobbies and Avocations

The following are pastime activities reported in the questionnaire or as I witnessed in our personal interaction during my advising them: sports, flying airplanes, reading about Buddhism, listening to music and meditating, studying science and space, martial arts, playing musical instruments, ballroom dancing, spending time with family, and spending time with friends.

Sources of the Greatest Influences (as of 2019)

Only three mentees responded: (1) "my father with his capacity to understand others," (2) "a few political friends," (3) "my fraternity advisor." Only these sources were identified, leading me to wondering if the remaining participants in the survey ever thought about those who may have had an influence on their lives.

Positive Mentor Qualities Identified by My Mentees

- empathy toward mentees (listening with empathy)
- knowledge in specific fields
- consistency between mentoring and practice
- values within realms of social responsibility
- resilience
- strong focus on guiding mentees

Organizational Memberships

- *Phi Sigma Kappa International Fraternity*
- *Club Regatas Lima*–Peru
- University Student Government Association, Greek Council, and Karate Club

- *Omicron Delta Kappa* (one-hundred-year-old national leadership honor society)
- sports clubs, a golf country club, Boy Scouts

Profession or Occupation (as of year 2019)

The mentees have been the following professionals:

- financial analysts, certified financial planner
- clinical psychologist
- business marketing specialist
- sports' coaches
- commercial underwriter with American Express
- certified public accountants
- owner of a children's educational video publishing company
- professors in the *La Universidad Nacional de Asunción* and members of the Paraguayan Legislature, Drs. Enrique Bendaña and Alfredo Ratti.

Greatest Strengths

The perceptions of multiple mentees regarding their personal strengths are reflected in four categories: (1) persistence in taking risks; (2) being a visionary; (3) trustworthiness, loyalty, risk-taking; and (4) resilience.

Greatest Weaknesses

Very few mentees reported weaknesses, but the following concepts seemed to reflect the feelings of the group: (1) impatience, (2) correcting children, (3) lack of tolerance, (4) excessive alcohol consumption, and (5) overeating.

Outstanding Personal Virtues

Many of my mentees considered these virtues a part of their lives: (1) friendship and loyalty, (2) caring about others and kindness, (3) leadership and tolerance, (4) hard work and tenaciousness, and (5) persistence and integrity.

Mentoring

What contributions did you see your mentors making to society?

They possess the following qualities:

- educator, mentor, teacher, professor
- makes a difference in the lives of others

- leaves a legacy
- excellent in international affairs and economics
- knows numerous foreign languages

Influences that Motivators Have Had on Mentees' Lives

The quotes reflect a few of the qualities that were duplicated by most of the respondents:

- "professional counsel and friendship"
- "elders, because my relationships with elders have changed my attitude positively and have helped me be stronger"
- "in my early childhood years, my father and maternal grandmother"

Persons You Most Admired

Many mentees generalized and referred to teachers and professors during their secondary and higher education. The following are specific:

- "Larry King, because I enjoyed his broadcasting and journalistic talents"
- Barack Obama, as the first Black President

- people who are humane and respect others' cultural differences
- fathers and grandfathers

Qualities of Successful Mentorship as Seen Through Mentees' Eyes

These qualities are a reflection of multiple mentees' experiences related to circumstances that surround the mentees during their growth into men:

- serves as a father image and friend
- helpful with emotions
- has integrity, dignity, and graciousness
- demonstrates unselfish behaviors
- exhibits problem-solving skills
- advises in career selections
- assists in transition from college to work
- tolerates errors and misfortunes
- shares wisdom through advice
- provides a feeling of safety and security
- delivers advice patiently
- uses examples and illustrations

- encourages, not just advises
- open to ideas and responses
- accepts negativity when necessary
- values personal relationships

Further Facts

I would be remiss in not discussing my experiences with young soldiers when I was an officer on active duty in the military in the mid-1950s. Most of them did not have bachelor's degrees, as they were young conscripted recruits. They were very curious about the world beyond their Military Occupational Specialty (MOS). In addition to their military obligations, they showed dedicated interests in their families and social activities. I found several with sexual problems and misunderstandings of sexual behavior, even conflicting with their religious backgrounds. They appeared to be good listeners and learners.

I will never forget one soldier. Peter, my chauffeur would shepherd me around in a jeep, talkative and curious about almost everything in life; he was particularly sensitive of his African American race. We had many sensitive conversations related to his experiences and his reactions to them.

Besides my usual assignments, I was also a member of the judicial arm as defense counsel for mostly AWOL soldiers. I learned the Uniform Code of Military Justice (UCMJ) and served my soldiers in the courts. Unintentionally, that was the beginning of my mentoring experiences, which carried me into a field far removed from my BS degree in accounting, although my exposure to military personnel began in my ROTC training at Loyola University of Chicago.

Summary Acknowledgment of Selected Mentees

There are several mentees I wish to acknowledge due to their unique lives. I consider it best to quote them with selected parts from their written responses in my questionnaire.

I. I lived in Santa Clara, Cuba, until November 1961, when I emigrated without my parents from whom I separated for eight years. I never lived with them again, as I moved to Texas and Louisiana, and my parents, brother and grandmother moved to Miami, FL. I went to a Catholic school in Cuba (Marist

Brothers) that gave me an excellent moral and academic education which served me well throughout my entire life. I spoke little English when I came to the USA. A miracle occurred, or was it a gift from a kind teacher, that I passed my Sophomore English class in high school. I moved to Hillsboro, Texas, as a Junior in the next semester year. During my Senior year, I was elected VP. This gave me confidence that served me well throughout the rest of my life. I lived in Texas with an uncle, a medical doctor, and his family. We were among the very few Spanish-speaking and Catholic families in the County then. I attended Hill Junior College where I was eventually Valedictorian of the graduating class. During my two years there, I majored in Economics and Political Science. I became the Vice President of the National Honor Society, Phi Theta Kappa. Then, I moved on to the University of Texas in Austin to complete my undergraduate degree, a B.A. in Economics, Spanish and Political Science. I remained at the university where I also received an MA in Latin America Studies-Economics, in 1983. This education changed my whole life and opened my eyes to the world, especially about Latin America. I received a Ph.D. in Political Science from the University of New Orleans in 1983.

In 1979, I was recruited by the Executive Director of the Inter-American Center at Loyola University in New Orleans. He was instrumental in promoting my professional interest. Later, I became President of Sonoma State University, in California where I remained for 24 years. In my retirement, I have returned to Austin Texas. My greatest achievement was serving as President of a university. I am President Emeritus and Professor Emeritus-Political Science. (At the time of this writing, 2019, I am 73 years old.) **Ruben Armiñana**

II. I have attended school from ages 5 through 29 with only an 18-month break and perhaps a weekend at a Catholic retreat focusing on spirituality and psychology. I was a good Catholic until I was 19. My religious interests are still Roman Catholicism. I have gone through many changes in my life. I knew I had strong drive and desire to succeed. My fraternity advisor was a professor at the university I attended; I quickly learned that he was great person. Later in life he became my best mentor, a relationship which ultimately developed into a strong friendship ... I am always surprised to hear that he continues to provide and encourage my fraternity brothers. He sets a high bar (tolerance and unconditional love) to which I aspire. **Anonymous**

III.I have been a student from ages 5 through 40, completing four post-graduate degrees. During a one 18-month break, I did some self-evaluation which included attending a Catholic retreat with my university undergraduate fraternity advisor. I demonstrated my interest in psychology during this time and during many consultations with my mentor. With his help, I realized that I was not yet ready to handle a four-year doctoral program, so I decided to pursue my MBA degree at Temple University Fox School of Business. My focus was to apply psychology in the context of organizing dynamics and leadership development. After completing my MBA, my mentor convinced me to enroll in a doctoral program in Psychology; I achieved a PsyD. in Clinical Psychology. Little did I ever imagine that I would eventually find my career as a psychotherapist. At this writing, I am a senior administrator in a large State Mental Institution. **Dr. Jeff Uhl**

IV. I was the third of 5 children (two older sisters, two younger brothers), raised under Catholic values, educated in a school in Chile staffed by Holy Cross Fathers, from Notre Dame, Indiana. Between 6 through 16 years of age, I spent two months summer holiday on my family's farm, 400 miles South of Santiago, Chile, surrounded by cousins and friends. I had the most rewarding outdoor experiences in a natural landscape, horseback riding, with fascinating anecdotes and knowledge from men cultivating the land and seeing the growth of forests. I had a routine life in Santiago, mainly spent in school learning with extra-curricular activities, plus with neighborhood friends, football games and later child-related activities. As an adult I extensively worked and traveled throughout the region.

My school sports were basketball, softball, high jump, and running. In elementary school I liked mostly biology. As an adult, I was engaged in social work with under- privileged people as members of *Obras Sociales Club, San Jorge, Chile*, which was staffed by school parents and alumni.

My mentor had the most impact on my life ... I would be remiss if I did not mention this mentor's role as one of my father figures ... I have been fortunate to have him in my lifetime; I modeled my life based on what I learned from this mentor. Of all the mentors I have had, this mentor leads the list. He selected me to join his staff at an American university; I had no teaching experiences, yet he saw in me a potential I had not realized. **Eduardo Besoain**

V. I did not have much interest in school until I went to college. From about Grades 3 through 12, I was bored. I began to have some interest in school when

I reached the 12th grade. I liked English Literature and Composition. A good female teacher encouraged me and helped me to discover my hidden, academic side. I always respected elders. I was more of an extrovert than introvert, although people sometimes called me shy, or a product of situational shyness, I suppose, yes, I was occasionally very playful. I was rational and emotional—medium on that continuum. I did not have an interest in athletics as I did not have athletic ability. I was small for my age and young for my grade placement. While growing up, I did very few chores around my home.

My mom sort of spoiled me. (My wife would agree with that.) I consider myself moral, as I attended church and practiced my religion. My father is a deacon in the Baptist Church, attends regularly, and still teaches Bible study. Yet, I did not like participating in church very much growing up, although I felt it as an obligation. I was probably hyperactive and hated to sit still. I maintained a close friendship with one person, although I liked being with my friends. I have good relationships with my siblings, then and today. **Anonymous**

VI.   Part of my daily challenge is struggling with who I was, who I am, and who I want to be—a battle within me is against myself; but I also realize that I'm no different than anyone else. I realize that I need God's grace to help me through this transition in life and one of the most beneficial has been through you (my mentor). **Richard Reisert**

VII.   My mentor was an "elderly man" in his late 40's when I was in my late 20's; we met in a university classroom, both taking a graduate course; my major was Psychology, and he advised me to take a second major in Business Administration—I greatly respected him and still do. **Richard Caudel**

VIII. I lost both my parents when I was in my late teens, which had a major impact on my life. This affected my growing up, my religion, family, profession, and interest in sports. My mother (43 years old) passed during a triple by-pass surgery when I was 16, and my father (at 47 years old) passed in a triple massive heart attack when I was 18 ... Through various loans, grants, and scholarships, I paid my own way through college. While in college, I confided in my mentor who was always there for me. He guided me in my pursuits, particularly in finding my career. **Dominic Callendriello**

Commentary

The review and compilation of multiple aspects of mentorship have reflected my mentees' values as young boys maturing into malehood.

- Developing oneself: "The self is not something ready-made, but something in continuous formation through choice of action" (John Dewey).
- Mentoring others: "A commonsense approach … that shows us all the benefits of reaching out to help someone else" (former congressman Joseph M. Hoeffel, US House of Representatives).
- Leaving a legacy: "When you were born, you cried and the world rejoiced; live your life so *that* when you die, the world cries and you rejoice" (White Elk).

The experiences enumerated throughout this book provide insight into my universe of mentees.

Chapter IV

Analysis

Based on my purpose in writing this book, which is to inspire my mentees' platform for their lives, I am now embarking on my perspective of this mentoring process. By so doing, I acknowledge that my mentees' behavioral and developmental factors have played a role in their relationships with other people. I have been overwhelmed to learn what my mentees have witnessed. They have honestly expressed themselves in their responses to my questionnaire, as presented in Chapter 3, as well as my discussions with them in relation to what I have carefully observed in their behavior.

My analytical remarks are appropriately related only to men. I have chosen not to conduct a comprehensive review of the literature on these subjects, as that would amount to an extensive search beyond the scope of my book. Besides, I do not indulge in elaboration of the subtopics below but only what I believe is sufficient to share my principal reflections. While I do not engage in psychological therapy with my mentees, most of them have known and felt that my mentoring renders specialized guidance beyond any professional help.

I do not hesitate to show that I have written many tautological expressions in my book, but in some instances, repetitions have been necessary with further explanations of the text. Regardless, I have tried to instill in my mentees that they should "Dream the impossible dream" (*from the Broadway show* Man of La Mancha).

I beg the readers' indulgence with my use of clichés, which I deem invaluable.

Nationalities

What do I say about nationalities? Surely, I recognize over many years, cultures have changed, just as national boundaries have changed in over 170 nations that have emerged. Historically, the world's peoples, with their distinct cultures, have automatically protected and respected themselves. In racial realities, ethnically, we find many subgroups: Hispanic, Palestinian, Slavic, mixed-races, mestizo, and numerous others. Anthropologists have summarized this concept as accidental by birth, not as preordained or preplanned. I did not experience any unusual or divergent behaviors based on the nationalities of my mentees although they were products of multiple national origins. Some showed machismo, or felt gender superiority, while others felt inferior to the women in their lives. This did not project any cause for variations in my mentoring style. Therefore, based on my mentee population, the differences in nationalities had relatively little effect on my ability to successfully interact with them.

Religion

The mentees' identification of their religion provides many variations found in the origins of their faiths and reflect their decisions to follow these religions. Some have offered their lack of belief in a God, and some are confused as to who that God may be: Yahweh, Jesus (Christ), Mohammad, Buddha, or others notably found in the Orient. Often in Western civilization, religions are referred to as primarily Judeo-Christian, yet there is atheism, as well as agnosticism. I have only mentored men who were of the Judeo-Christian and Islamic faiths.

After many occasions in conversations with my mentees, religious concepts entered our discussions. I found that as young men, some rejected religious expression and shied away from following their faith because their behaviors did not support their religious principles. As they grew older, they began to reach for the support that religion can offer and felt that they reached a higher level of maturity. At that point, our discussion bases changed, and we communicated on different levels.

According to Wilkins, religion is valuable in human behavior and beliefs. Wilkins writes this:

> We wonder what it is, and why it is, and whether it is natural to people, and whether it is really for us. And eventually, we all take a stance concerning religion … Why is this so?

Perhaps the first reason is sociological. People experience religion around them, see it in action, and wonder why it is part of human experience.

The second reason seems to be experiential. People who have been brought up in a particular religion wonder about it. They ask what it really means, where it came from, why they belong to this religious community rather than that.

Another reason that people wonder about religion in their lives it might be called "influential." They see many people who practice no religion, experience a disdain for religion in certain segments of society.

But perhaps the most important reason that people ask themselves about religion and its role in their own lives is that thoughtful people wonder about the meaning of life. (Wilkins, pp. 4–5)

Religion is often defined as *faith* or *belief.* In *Latin*, it is called *Credo.* My simple definition is that religion is the tie that binds man to God.

The following thoughts are confirmations of what I have learned from my mentees. Our modern society has ushered a new pattern of relationships that cross religious boundaries. Many of my mentees have married outside of their birth religion and reflect a social change that intermarriage and child raising have altered. Their faith has taken on a different hue in some cases that leads them on a pilgrimage beyond their youth.

According to Rokeach,

> *Faith* refers to one or more beliefs a person accepts as true, good, or desirable, regardless of social consensus or objective evidence, which are perceived as irrelevant. A *delusion* is a belief on faith judged by an external observer to have no objective basis and which is in fact, wrong. A *stereotype* is a socially shared belief that describes an attitude in an oversimplified or undifferentiated manner; an attitude object

is said to prefer certain modes of conduct …
(p. 125) … All organized western religious
groups teach their adherents and those they
try to convert, contradictory sets of beliefs.
On the other hand, they each have mutual
love and respect, and the Golden Rule, the
love of justice and equality of all men in the
eyes of God. On the other hand, they teach
(implicitly if not openly) that certain people
can be saved—those who believe as they do;
that certain people are chosen people; that
theirs is the only truth. (p. 189)

As I have seen, while observing men, their religion
appears more therapeutic than their belief in any God;
many find religion to be a relief from distress, perhaps
increasing their self-confidence.

I do not want to sound theological, but I believe we all
acknowledge the same God, whether it be Yahweh, Jesus,
Allah, or any oriental being who leads to the Omnipotent.

Morality

Although some of these men consider religion as solely a guide to moral behavior, I usually do not agree. Stewart best confirms my understanding that "The reason for the unconditional character of the moral imperative is that it puts our essential being as a demand against us" (p. 396). The practice of morality is often viewed through religious symbols; thus, some mentees have rejected those symbols. I have often reiterated to my mentees that their sensitivity may bring them closer to God.

Today's lack of moral leadership jeopardizes democracy and the future of these mentees and their families. Nancy Gibbs, director of Harvard's Shorenstein Center laments that "in our schools and sanctuaries and clubs and communities, in our dealings with alienated friends and family, the vital work of replacing toxic fantasies with hard realities ..." (p. 18) has presented society with the challenge unlike ever before. These men must be prepared to address threats with the sense of moral courage as their strength.

Education

As my mentees have shown in my questionnaire in Chapter 3, their levels of education range from the lower rung of the ladder to higher steps on the ladder. I passionately believe that education begins at home as a child. Thus, life continues with or without any formal education. But with education in schools, particularly in colleges, one develops a different perspective on life, which often leads to unexpected careers or professions.

I have impressed upon my mentees that securing an academic degree or achieving a particular level of education is the bottom rung on the ladder, but how one climbs that ladder and uses his knowledge to conduct his life is critical.

> *Education is the most powerful*
> *weapon which can be used to*
> *change the world.*
> *—Nelson Mandela*

As we have witnessed among great leaders, their contribution to society is measured by examples and results more than through academic principles, such as Mahatma

Gandhi, Abraham Lincoln, Margaret Thatcher, Golda Meir, Simón Bolívar.

Family

Children are biologically and psychologically linked to parents based on gender and size of family. Relationships generally foster love, affection, and devotion. I suppose we can say that family members engage in sharing knowledge and behaviors, along with personal attributes. I have discussed with my mentees about how they fit into their families and what they feel as their role in that environment. On many occasions, their masculine identification in the role of son, brother, grandson, or uncle all revolves around individual relationships based on current family and ancestry. Many mentees focus proudly on the origins of their families or their ancestries. Their reflections and attention to the mores of their families influence a large part of their behaviors.

In his book *Sharing Wisdom: The Practical Art of Giving and Receiving Mentoring*, Wicks writes this:

Recently a colleague and I were enjoying a conversation about an article on psychoanalysis published in the *New Yorker*. We both found it intriguing and humorous. ... at the end of the article I filled up and cried. When the writer shared his feelings about the death of his analyst, I thought of my own losses. (p. 15)

Through my observation of my mentees, I found some of them doubted how shared experiences would serve a positive result. Why was this so? Perhaps it was related to gender and personality.

Perhaps sharing events serves as a positive experience between father and son rather than mother and son. "Men should feel obligated to engage in their fatherhood, not just spectate ... mother can't fully connect with her pubescent son in the same way a man can't fully connect with his daughter when she experiences her first menstrual cycle" (Epps, p. 9). See more on this topic under the heading "Fatherhood."

Culture

As I have read in my mentees' statements about culture, they seem to have many misunderstandings or unclear definitions of the term *culture*. According to Brooks in *The Social Animal*, culture itself is "a collection of habits, practices, beliefs, arguments, and tensions that regulates and guides human life. Culture transmits certain practical solutions to everyday problems—how to avoid poisonous plants, how to form successful family structures" (pp. 148-149).

Brooks expands the characteristics of culture as a product of the following: "racial and ethnic backgrounds, nationalities, languages, ages, maturity, friendship, personal situations, organizational customs and capital structure, intellectual IQ, association with some persons like their peers, family or tribal norms." With reference to traits that are correlated to success, Brooks also identifies "attention to details, persistency, efficiency, analytical thoroughness, and the ability to work long hours" (p. 137). Within each culture there are multiple components such as religions, languages, and physical characteristics.

Another aspect of culture deals with one's emotions as reflective of such attractions as holidays, symbols, works of art, and other types of "implicit and often unnoticed messages" that influence "how to feel, how to respond, and how-to divine meanings" (Scruton, p. 116).

These represent what I have noticed and what I have heard expressed by the mentees on a conscious level when they realized how their subconscious adjusted for these differences. In this sense, my mentees have described their adaptations to various culture differences.

Contributions to Society

In my discussion with my mentees regarding their contributions to society, most of them felt their influence on clients, patients, customers, and students related to their professional expertise rather than personal influence. Further, any contributions often resulted from the mentees' activities with groups. Some recognized that the results of contributions emanated from their ethical behavior. Stewart presents excerpts from C. S. Lewis: "We do not observe men, we are *men*. In this case, so to speak, men find themselves under a moral law, which they did not make" (p.107). Hence, morals and ethics often play a major part in mentees' identification of their personal contributions.

Catastrophes

My mentees described many situations that developed in their lives. Some difficult problems related to their divorces and caused their separation from their sons who might eventually grow up without a male image. "It's not at all easy to deprogram oneself from deep-rooted messages about parenthood" (Epps, p. 53). I believe young boys can be imprisoned by their own inhibitors, which could amount to catastrophes, sometimes perceived more than real. I have tried often to impress on my mentees that catastrophes, like disappointments or mental depression, can be blessings in disguise; in other words, depression is not always an enemy but can be an awakening to a new reality. Also, one's faith can positively change behaviors.

Some mentees had major catastrophes, such as nervous breakdowns due to serious drug addictions. To the best of my memory, none was hospitalized because of this situation. I always endeavored to give them my best advice as a sincere mentor, but I advised them to seek psychotherapy, hopefully to arrive at a better understanding of reality.

I spent time with one mentee hospitalized with a brain tumor from which he did not survive. I found it important, regardless of the circumstances, to offer my comfort.

Attitude

Attitude has multiple definitions; it represents a way of thinking and observing things that can vary and change. It can be used to describe a behavior, or it can be a behavior itself. An attitude displays a sense of arrogance and egotism, a virtual chip on his shoulder. In my mentoring, I have found that as boys grow older, their attitudes seem to reveal different human behaviors, some positive but, occasionally, some negative. Certain boys and men developed superiority complexes, others inferiority, while others fluctuated depending on circumstances. As a mentor, I saw the attitudes that would detract from their personalities, and I addressed their behavior the only way I knew how: talking as a friend and as a father.

Creativity

Surely, I have witnessed many talents revealed through the initiatives of my mentees. I believe the results are a product of desire combined with an open mind, along with talent that I dare call meta-reality or self-awareness.

> Picasso inherited the traditions of Western Art, but he also responded to the mask of African art ... In *Les Demoiselles d'Arvignon,* Picasso's fantastic burst of creativity (Brooks, p. 156).

I have admonished my mentees to avoid overindulging in too much imagination despite the level of their IQ. They need a balance between creativity and realism.

Strengths and Weaknesses

The mentees had a variety of attributes related to strengths and weakness, yet they considered their risk-taking as part of their lives. Some considered taking risks as a strength, while others felt it was a weakness, depending upon circumstances. Some of my mentees have implied that they approved of taking risks, such as investing in the stock market. That type of risk was a strength. I have often told my mentees that the best investments they make should be encouraging their children to learn a trade or seek more formal education in college; their children are their best investments.

Neither in my questionnaire nor through my discussions with them over the years was I able to observe any levels of humility. "Humility, rather than being weak or defenseless, is the powerful counterattack to the enemy. In the secular ideal of strength and self-sufficiency, to have a weakness, much less to acknowledge it as such, is contrary to maturity. But in the warfare of spiritual maturity, humility is the strongest weapon in your arsenal" (Aschenbrenner, p. 187). Refer to my description of Aschenbrenner in Chapter 1. To me, *humility* is a virtue that my mentees have seldom revealed about themselves. Further, I tried to display my own sense of humility as I interacted with them, but I doubt if they perceived it.

As the future is unknown, a *faux pas* is realistic and becomes a general challenge for successful social behavior. I support that my mentees reach into their arsenal of strength to overcome their weaknesses.

Fatherhood

The concept of father-and-son relationships is indeed complex, as most sociologists agree. I have found that several of my mentees looked at fatherhood as a condition of having mutual respect and obligations between father and son. Sometimes boys put halos on their fathers, thus revealing their deep emotional ties.

In his book *From Fatherless to Fatherhood,* Omar Epps shows that fatherhood has a strong correlation with races. "Fatherhood in America is a complex issue, and yet it shouldn't be, though it's almost impossible to address it effectively without discussing race" (Epps, p .80). Among my mentees of all races and religions, race and religion have never been an issue.

As a corollary, often "machismo gets in the way of male relationships, with either father or son. The boy may not comprehend his role in the family nor with his male friends. Understanding 'machismo' may best be described as 'synonymous with *hypermasculinity,*' an overemphasis on traditional masculine traits" (Garfield, p. 37). Thus, consequences arise, causing boys' subconscious rifts with fathers. This relationship has a prominent place within my mentees' experiences.

Commentary

Several of My Major Thoughts

As I worked with my mentees, I consistently recognized my obligation to leave with them the following:

1. To remember the many days of their early lives as young boys, both the positive and negative
2. To avoid excessive anger, which may cause unwelcomed anxiety
3. To remember their moral compass
4. To seek justice and correct oppression (Isaiah 1:17)
5. To believe in a Supreme Being whose *will* is greater than man's desires.

Whereas some of us come from country roads and others come from city streets, once we were little boys regardless of the paths we have taken. As my mentees have witnessed many problems and endured all kinds of distress, most have matured and reached their respective goals. My experiences with my mentees have been an interconnection that I will never forget. I am grateful as a handyman of God.

Genius is the power of carrying the feelings
of manhood into the powers of manhood.
—*Samuel Taylor Coleridge*

Conclusion

This experience in mentoring men has been a daunting opportunity in my life. I would be remiss in not sharing my nationalities—German, French, Irish, and Arabic, all of which have served me well in my contributions to this endeavor. Certainly, my Louisiana Creole culture, with a mixture of my multiple ethnic backgrounds, provides me with an understanding of the demands of different environments and family structures that has enlarged my scope when I provided advice to my mentees; we have shared our aspirations and goals, along with our respective values.

This mentoring experience has provided me with a trove of information. Likewise, I consider it to be a golden standard of my life. As I review my analysis in Chapter 4, the grace of God has been my enlightenment. I admit that the COVID-19 pandemic of 2020–2021, while painstaking, has caused some stress in my preparing the final segments of this book; nevertheless, I have not allowed it to reduce my fortitude and energies.

This conclusion does not suggest that other writers in this field may not have carved their versions of masculinity. I do not claim my work here to approach any seminal values. Finally, readers may find that most chapters show my intentions to serve as inspiration for boys and matured male adults to seek ways of building a stronger future. Together, my mentees and I have traveled over many roads and crossed the trails covered by our footprints.

Finale

My book could not have been possible without the dedication and assistance of my in-house editor and devoted, lovely wife, Nina Joy. As a professional writer, she collaborated with the publishing editor. We reside in a senior resident community (Ann's Choice) in Warminster, Pennsylvania.

We have seven adult children, four American born, two Middle Eastern born Muslin Arabs whom we met in Amman, Jordan, when we both taught at the University of Jordan in 1992, and one son born in South America, whom we met in Quito, when we taught at the University of Ecuador in 1999. Our family represents a combined set of cultures and use of multiple languages.

Our pleasure has found no end with this family of seven who embody the principals explored in this book.

Ad Majorem Dei Gloriam

"All for the greater glory of God."

(Source: Society of Jesus, S.J.)

References

Allen, James. (2019). *As A Man Thinketh*. New York, NY: St. Martin's Essential Press.

Angelou, Maya. (1971). *I Know Why the Caged Bird Sings*. Bantam Books.

Aschenbrenner, George, SJ. (2004). *Stretched for Greater Glory*. Chicago, IL: Loyola Press.

Bertstein, Elizabeth. *Strategies for Raising Boys, Bonds on Relationship*.

Brooks, David. (2001). *The Social Animal—Hidden Sources of Love, Character, and Achievement*. New York, NY: Random House Publishing Group.

Calloway, Donald H. (2010). *No Turning Back—A Witness to Mercy*. Stockbridge, MA: Marian Press.

Costello, Brian J. (2010). *A History of Pointe Coupe'e Parish, Louisiana*. Donaldsonville, LA: Margaret Media Inc.

Covey, Stephen R. (2016). *An Effective Life—Inspiration about Effectiveness*. New York, NY: Mjf Books.

Culbertson, Phillip L., ed. (1884). *The Spirituality of Men—Sixteen Christians Write about Their Faith*. Minneapolis, MN: Annsbur Press.

Epps, Omar. (2018). *From Faithless to Fatherhood*. Lulu Publishing Services.

Evely, Louis. (1964). *That Man Is You*. Westminster, Maryland: The Newman Press.

Friday, Nancy. (1980). *Men in Love: Men's Sexual Fantasies: The Triumph of Love over Rage*. New York, NY: Delacorte Press.

Garfield, Robert. (2015). *Breaking the Male Code— Unlocking the Power of Friendship*. New York, NY: Penguin Random House.

Gibbs, Nancy. (2021). America's Moral Vacuum. *Time,* February 8, p. 18.

Greeley, Andrew M. (2001). *My Love: A Prayer Journal*. Franklin, WI: Sheed & Ward.

Haydel, Belmont F. (2004). *A Rendezvous with My Professional Destiny—Making a Difference*. USA: Xlibris Publishing.

Hero, Basil. *The Mission of a Lifetime—Lessons from the Men Who Went to the Moon*.

James, David C. (1996). *What Are They Saying about Masculine Spirituality?* Mahwah, NJ: Paulist Press.

Kendall, Joshua. (2016). *First Dads*. New York, NY: Grand Central Publishing.

Malone, Mathew, SJ. The Pilgrim. *America Magazine,* November 11, 2019, p. 3.

Merton, Thomas. (1948). *Seven Storey Mountain*. Brace and Javanovich.

Milstein, Richard. (1999). *The Sexual Male—Problems and Solutions*. New York, NY: W. W. Norton.

Monynihan, Robert. (2013). *Recen por Mí* (translation from Italian to Spanish) about Pope Francis.

Moore, Thomas. (2000). *Care of the Soul—a Guide for Cultivating Depth and Sacredness in Everyday Life*. New York, NY: HarperCollins Publishers Inc. ISBN:-0-06- 06597-9.

Newberger, Eli H. (1999). *The Men They Will Become—the Nature and Nurture of Male Character*. Da Capo Press.

Northrup, Solomon. (1970). *Twelve Years a Slave*. Mineola, NY: Dover Publications.

Ornstein, Peggy. (2020). Miseducation of the American Boy. *The Atlantic*, January/February, p. 66.

Philin, Regis, and Bill Zephine. (1955). *I'm Only One Man!* New York, NY: Hyberion Publishers.

Rokeach, Milton. (1968). *Beliefs, Attitudes, and Values: A Theory of Organization and Change.* San Francisco, CA: Lossey-Bass Inc.

Sanford, John A. (1988). *What Men Are Like.* Mahwah, NJ: Paulist Press.

Stewart, David. (sec. ed. 1988). *Exploring the Philosophy of Religion.* Englewood Cliffs, NJ: Prentice Hall.

Wicks, Robert J. (2000). *Sharing Wisdom—the Practical Art of Giving and Receiving Mentoring.* New York, NY: The Crossroads Publishing Company.

Wilkins, Ronald J. *Religions of the World.* Dubuque, Iowa: W. C. Brown Publishers.

Acknowledgments

The following persons have contributed or influenced my preparation of this book. Each professional, in his or her own way, offered me encouragement and guidance. I respect their experience and personal observations in their varied fields, and I appreciate their contributions.

Ashraf Al-Shihabi, CPA

Ashraf is a Certified Public Accountant (CPA) licensed in the Commonwealth of Virginia and District of Columbia, a Certified Fraud Examiner (CFE), and a Chartered Financial Analyst (CFA-level 1). He holds two master's degrees, one in accountancy from Rider University and the other one in banking and financial sciences with distinction/honors, and currently is pursuing his Juris Master (JM) degree from

Scalia Law School at George Mason University. Throughout his career, he has held several leadership and executive positions, including experienced Manager of Financial Reporting Disputes and Monitorship, Senior Accounting Manager, and Controller and Director of Finance.

Joy Allingham, Educator

Joy is an educator with a passion for making students feel welcome and valued in and out of her classroom setting. As part of the Rider University family, she has taught ESL classes and composition classes and supervised the academic program for Study Tours, an international study program. Joy's educational background includes MA in educational leadership from Saint Mary's College in Moraga, California, and a BS in art education from Pennsylvania State University. She is currently an adjunct instructor at Rider University and has experience as an educational consultant, high school principal, and high school teacher of world history, English, and graphic arts.

Anthony Angeli, Marketing and Consumer Packaging Specialist

Anthony is a graduate of Rider University with a degree in business administration, which includes marketing and communications. He has made a career as a consumer packaged goods (CPG) professional. Anthony's leadership skills were honed in his early Phi Sigma Kappa fraternity days at Rider University, which extended to its New Jersey alumni chapter and philanthropic work. He continues to enjoy the benefits of team sports as a state- and nationally certified soccer and basketball official at the youth and scholastic level.

Kenneth John (Jack) Barber Jr., PhD, Psychologist

Dr. Barber is a graduate of William Penn Charter School in Philadelphia. He received a BA degree from Dickinson College in Carlisle, Pennsylvania, and received a PhD in psychology from Temple University. Dr. Barber was director of adult outpatient services at Northeast Community Center for Behavioral Health and was senior staff psychologist at Friends Hospital. He and Dr. Ernst Schmidt of Gloria Dei Church in Huntingdon Valley cofounded the Growth

Opportunity Center, one of the largest outpatient mental health services in the Greater Philadelphia region. Dr. Barber is a past president of the Philadelphia Society of Clinical Psychologists.

Dominick Callendriello, Entrepreneur and Industry Strategic Adviser

Dominick, a graduate of Rider University, is a proven entrepreneur and business leader with a history of managing and growing technology organizations. He has over twenty-five years of experience in leveraging technology solutions that drive innovation and productivity in enterprise environments. He is a builder and manager of teams that provide customer service and support to business clients as well as a communications technology and cybersecurity consultant to business executives and IT department stakeholders. In his field, he is a strategic adviser to enterprise technology vendors and service providers and is frequently quoted by journalists as an industry and channel sales expert.

Laurel Ginsburgh, PhD, Speech-Language Pathologist

Dr. Ginsburgh holds an undergraduate degree from George Washington University in Washington, DC, and master of science degree and PhD from Columbia University in speech-language pathology, and she has taught at Rutgers University and Wilkes University. She was a speech pathologist at the Brooklyn VA Hospital in New York.

John (Bill) Haydel Jr., Retired Educator, Coach

John, an active successful educator, served for over thirty-seven years as teacher, athletic coach, administrator, and chief administrator in schools with a wide range of sizes and diverse ethnic and socioeconomic groups. He received a BS in mathematics, MA in school administration from California State University, a counseling certification from Chapman College, and additional certification in physical education from Pepperdine University. He was certified as a coach and attended the Character Counts! program and Pursuing Victory with Honor workshops. He was a member of the National Federation of State High School Associations and a member of the Nike Coaches Network, among many other coaching organizations.

Haller Ramos de Freitas, Exporter/Importer Entrepreneur

Haller works and lives in São Paulo, Brazil. He received a law degree from the *Universidade de São Paulo* in Brazil. He has worked in international law with UNESCO, International Court of Human Rights in Strarbourgh, and the Hague Academy of International Law, in private law and public law. After some years, he moved into the field of commerce and founded ProSwim, a swimming product company that had been a supplier and sponsor of Rio's 2016 Olympic Games, along with a noted Brazilian confederation and several South American federations. He is also a CEO along with his partner in Myrtha Brasil and CIMAI Brasil, two companies connected with swimming.

Rich Reisert, Investment Counselor

Rich received his BS in finance from Rider University. He has over thirty-five years of experience in the investment industry. He started his career with Hamilton & Co. as a global investment advisor with Mercer Investment Consulting. Following his career, Rich was a principal and director of management research at Bank of America

Securities. He later moved into a senior marketing and client service investment role at Phoenix Investment Partners. Currently, he is a managing member, principal and chief operating officer at Christenson Investment Partners. Rich has written several articles on finance and investments, including one published for the Investment Management Consultants Association.

Bernard Roseman, Retired Attorney

Atty. Roseman, BS engr., MBA, JD, began his career as an engineer and performed as project manager on the Pioneer satellite, the first satellite to orbit Jupiter and Saturn and leave our solar system. Later, he joined an engineering firm as vice president, chief administrative officer, and corporate counsel. He has served as vice president and member of the board of directors of several not-for-profit corporations and as management consultant to numerous nonprofit corporations. He is a member of the State Bar of California.

Jeff Uhl, PsyD, Industrial and Clinical Psychologist

Dr. Uhl received his BS in business administration (major: finance) from Rider University and MBA from Temple University's Fox School of Business. He completed his PsyD in clinical psychology at the Philadelphia College of Osteopathic Medicine and has a successful career where he combines his training in business and clinical psychology. He is currently deputy chief executive officer and practicing psychologist at the Ann Klein Forensic Center in New Jersey. He is an active member of the American Psychological Association. During his time working at one of New Jersey's civil commitment hospitals, Dr. Uhl and his team won the Governor Codey Award in the first statewide competition for improving mental health services in the state of New Jersey. The project focused on reducing restraints and staff injuries using Lean Six Sigma management principles.

Endorsements

Ehab Al-Shihabi, CPA

I was in my final year at the University of Jordan, living in Amman, Jordan, with little money but with huge ambition. I was always searching for an opportunity to grow. One day I heard that a Fulbright professor joined the faculty of Business School in my final year. I walked into his office and introduced myself to Professor Haydel. This was the turning point in my life. We got to know each other, and he accepted me as a son. He arranged for me to come to the United States and live in his home. He also arranged for me to secure a consulting job with KMPG in New York City and continues coaching, supporting, advising my career, my life, and my destiny. Living as his son and sharing meals with him enabled me to see how tirelessly he worked spending hours helping students and young underprivileged professionals to find their calling. I was one of them. I enjoyed an amazing journey with Dr. Belmont Haydel and absorbed his wisdom, experience, and knowledge. I have kept my promise to share his wisdom with my friends, family, and others. Because of him, I am a proud student at the Fletcher School for Law and Diplomacy pursuing my Ph.D. Simply put, Professor Haydel was not only a teacher or professor to me, but he was also a mentor, a coach, an advisor, and above all, my American father with a tremendous integrity and wisdom whom I will always admire.

Richard Caudel, President and CEO, Rock 'N Learn Inc.

Sometimes we are fortunate to encounter that rare individual who changes the course and purpose of our life in profound ways. For me that person was Belmont Haydel. We became friends during a graduate class in organizational psychology in 1978. I was drawn to Belmont's insightful comments, especially about the social responsibility of corporations.

Belmont shared his vast experiences as a retired Army Major, U.S. diplomat, and other government service work. I honestly had no idea how Belmont's wisdom, example, and expertise would change my life and my ability to serve others. I was graduated and formed my own company to help meet the educational needs of school children around the world, combining all aspects of my education. I have enjoyed many successes over the past 34 years while influencing millions of lives in my own way. Without Belmont's mentoring, I am certain none of this would have happened.

Thomas Reigert, Former US Diplomat

Belmont Haydel has been a close friend since we served in the Economic Section of the American Embassy in Buenos Aires in 1967. The high regard which Argentine officials and other Latin American businessmen had for Belmont was clear from the start, and their effusive praise of his commitment to American relations—North and South—spoke volumes. His continuous mentoring of those with whom he worked was evident through his thoroughness in providing information, and his helping others navigate required procedures; this was unlike anything they had known before. Moreover, the natural warm and human manner in which Belmont related to the generally formal *Porteño* demonstrated formidable diplomatic skills. These qualities have stood him well in his academic career, which included the Executive Directorship of the Inter-American Center at Loyola University in New Orleans, sponsored and funded by USAID. This position included training potential Latin American leaders in community leadership, a passion that Belmont has been committed to during his entire professional career, in all its many facets. Belmont's contributions to practical scholarship and higher education have been exemplified by the way he has instilled common humanity into his business associates, colleagues, and students.

NOTES

Index

H

Haydel, Belmont, Sr., 2

humility, 72

I

Inter-American Center (IAC), xiii, 6, 98, 100

J

Johnson, Lyndon B., 5

K

Kennedy, John F., 5

L

lack of moral leadership, 63

leadership abilities, 11, 13

M

manhood, 9–10

manliness, 12

masculinity, 9–12, 26

  mentees' views, 12

McDonald, Alton, 3

mentees, xviii

mentoring, xviii–xix

mentoring experience, 76–77

morality, 63

N

nationalities, 57

O

Orenstein, Peggy, 26

  "The Miseducation of the American Boy," 26

P

personal reflections

  answers regarding early memories, 31

  catastrophes, 34

  contributions to society, 38, 68

  cultural activities, 37

  education, 36

  greatest achievements, 39

  greatest strengths and weaknesses, 41

  hobbies and avocations, 39

  influences of motivators, 43

  inhibiting factors, 35

  mentees' most admired persons, 43

  mentor qualities, 42

  mistakes, 32–33

  organizational memberships, 40

  personality, 31, 36

  positive mentor qualities, 40

  professions, 41

  qualities of successful mentorship, 44

  sources of greatest influences, 40

  virtues, 42

Lightning Source UK Ltd.
Milton Keynes UK
UKHW041847030521
383075UK00008B/681/J